INFORMATION
EXPLORER
JUNIOR

Watch It!
Researching
with Videos

by Kristin Fontichiaro

CHERRY LAKE PUBLISHING · ANN ARBOR, MICHIGAN

CHERRY LAKE Publishing

Published in the United States of America
by Cherry Lake Publishing
Ann Arbor, Michigan
www.cherrylakepublishing.com

Content Adviser: Gail Dickinson, PhD, Professor,
Old Dominion University, Norfolk, Virginia

Photo Credits: Cover, ©Monkey Business Images/Shutterstock.com; page 8,
©Maros Bauer/Shutterstock.com; page 11, ©RimDream/Shutterstock.com;
page 16, ©John McCormick/Shutterstock.com; page 18, ©wavebreakmedia/
Shutterstock.com

Library of Congress Cataloging-in-Publication Data
Fontichiaro, Kristin.
  Watch it! : researching with videos / by Kristin Fontichiaro.
    pages cm. — (Information explorer junior)
  Includes bibliographical references and index.
  ISBN 978-1-63188-863-2 (lib. bdg.) — ISBN 978-1-63188-875-5 (pbk.) —
ISBN 978-1-63188-887-8 (pdf) —ISBN 978-1-63188-899-1 (e-book)
  1. Research—Audio-visual aids—Juvenile literature. 2. Video recordings—
Juvenile literature. 3. Research—Methodology—Juvenile literature. I. Title.

  ZA4575.F66 2015
  001.4'2—dc23   2014032316

Cherry Lake Publishing would like to acknowledge the work of The Partnership
for 21st Century Skills. Please visit www.p21.org for more information.

Printed in the United States of America
Corporate Graphics Inc.
January 2015

Table of Contents

CHAPTER ONE

Using Video for Research

When you think about **research**, what do you imagine? You might think of gathering information by reading. Videos are another great way to learn information for your projects. A good informational video can bring your **topics** to life. You can hear what it sounds like when a lion roars and find out how long the roar lasts. You can even see Mount Rushmore up close or watch a high-speed train whoosh by.

Just like reading books or articles, you need to look for details and important information as you watch videos. You also need to keep your ears open and listen to the video's sound. This book will give you **strategies** for learning as much as you can from videos.

To get a copy of this activity, visit www.cherrylakepublishing.com/activities.

Try This

Before you start looking for videos, you will need a research topic. What do you want to learn about? A good research topic is something you are a little familiar with but want to know more about. Set a timer for 2 minutes. How many research topics can you think of?

When you are done, try **ranking** the topics. Put a star next to your favorite two topics.

CHAPTER TWO

Starting a Search

You can't search for videos if you don't know anything about your topic. Start by reading an encyclopedia entry or a short book about your topic. Keep a list of important words, people, or ideas. You can use these as search terms when you look for videos.

Search terms are the words people type in order to find the information they are looking for. You need good search terms to find the right videos for your project.

For example, Andre was eating a box of his favorite crackers. He saw a cheetah drawn

on the package. That made him curious to learn more about cheetahs. He read an encyclopedia entry about cheetahs. Then he decided to look for a video.

Andre started by simply typing the topic into the search box of his **browser**:

SEARCH: cheetah

Notice how Andre typed "cheetah" even though he is interested in "cheetahs." Using the simplest version of the word will give the best results. Typing "cheetah" will give results about both a "cheetah" and many "cheetahs." The plural word has the singular word within it, so the Internet searches for both words. But typing "cheetahs" would miss any site using only the word "cheetah."

For most topics, just searching the topic is enough. But some topics might give you too many results to sort through. Andre got so many results when he searched "cheetah" that he couldn't pick which videos to watch. He decided to add words that could narrow his search:

SEARCH: baby cheetah

SEARCH: cheetah eating

SEARCH: cheetah running

Seeing a cheetah in motion explains its movements better than words could.

These searches helped Andre find videos of the exact things he wanted to see. Notice that he added more words but not many. When you look for written information on Web sites, you might use several words in a search. Here's a tip, though. When you are looking for videos, you will get more results by using fewer words in your search. This is because people don't use many words to describe the videos they post online. So this search:

SEARCH: baby cheetah

is almost always going to result in more videos than:

What do baby cheetahs eat when they are born?

It seems weird, but it works! Some search sites can guess what you mean if you misspell a word. Others cannot. It's a good idea to check your spelling with an adult or someone else with good spelling skills if you aren't getting the results you expect.

To get a copy of this activity, visit www.cherrylakepublishing.com/activities.

Try This

Read an encyclopedia entry or a picture book about your topic. As you read, write down some key words and ideas. Use them as you work on your searches! Try to list mostly nouns. These are people, places, things, and ideas. For example, here are some keywords you might write down while reading about space travel.

moonwalk
space shuttle
satellite
neil armstrong

Notice that you don't need to capitalize Neil Armstrong's name in your search. Even though you should use capital letters for names when you write, you can use lowercase letters when you search!

CHAPTER THREE

Finding Videos

Now you have some strategies for searching.
But where should you go to find videos? And
how do you know which videos are best for
your project? Some online sources are better
than others for different topics. Knowing
where to look will give you better results!

There are so many videos online that choosing the
right ones can be the hardest part of your research.

Your Classroom or Library

Sometimes the best places to start searching are the shelves and Web sites of your school library, public library, or classroom. A library might offer its members free access to video sites such as BrainPop.com or DiscoveryEducation.com. These sites have great videos, but they usually cost money. The library might also have DVDs that you can check out.

Sites About Topics

A great way to find high-quality videos is to search on sites that are devoted to specific topics. Here are some good sites to search for popular elementary school topics:

Space: www.nasa.gov/multimedia/videogallery

Animals: http://video.nationalgeographic.com/video/animals

Math: www.khanacademy.org ← (ask your teacher or parent to sign in for you)

YouTube and Vimeo

You have probably used YouTube, the Web's largest collection of videos. Vimeo is another very popular video site. Anyone can make and share videos on these sites. This means you can find videos about anything. The bad news is that some of these videos might have been made by people who don't know much about your topic. They could have false information. In addition, some videos aren't meant for kids your age. Ask an adult for help if you're not sure if a video is right for you.

SchoolTube.com and TeacherTube.com

Many of the videos on these sites were made by teachers. Others were made by students who had help from their teachers. Any of them could be useful, but the ones made by teachers are often the most helpful.

Google.com or Bing.com

You can also use a regular **search engine** to look for videos. Type in your search carefully: use few words, no questions, and good spelling.

When the search engine returns its list of results, find the word "videos" at the top of the screen and click on it. You will now see a list of videos that match your search.

Once you are on the videos page, there will be a number next to each video, like this: 4:48

Does this mean "4:48 p.m."? No! It means that the video is 4 minutes and 48 seconds long. So a video that is 28:42 will take almost half an hour to watch. Before you click, think about how much time you want to spend watching.

To get a copy of this activity, visit www.cherrylakepublishing.com/activities.

Try This

Use the keywords you listed in chapter two to try different searches about your topic. Pick a few videos that seem good. Write down the search terms you used, the URL (Web address), and the length of each video.

Now watch the beginning of each video. Note why it is helpful. Does it answer questions you had about the topic? Is it filled with facts that you didn't know before? These are some signs of a good video. If a video doesn't seem helpful in the first few minutes, skip it and go on to another one!

Organize your information like this:

Search Terms	URL	Length	Why It Will Help with My Research
ford mustang	www.ford.com/cars/mustang	Doesn't say	Official Web site for Ford Mustang
ford mustang	www.youtube.com/watch?v=vasnZT9kf6c	8:34	Gives a tour of the 2015 Mustang. Shows what it looks like. Guy from Ford does the tour.
mustang race car	www.youtube.com/watch?v=vrE72iCqpVY	3:50	Shows what the race car version looks like

CHAPTER FOUR

Making Notes

Now the fun really begins. You are going to watch videos and gather information.

Great researchers know that they can't remember everything when they are learning about a topic. Instead, they write down information one piece at a time. They also make notes about where they found each

Lake Superior borders the northern side of Michigan.

piece of information. This is helpful in case they want to go back and look at it again.

When you are taking notes on a video, you should watch it at least twice. This will help you capture the details. Some people take notes both times they watch. Others watch the first time without writing and then make notes the second time. Keep watching over and over until you have all of the information you need.

You can save time when you take notes by writing down only the most important words. Natasha wanted to learn about the Great Lakes. She watched one video that said, "Four Great Lakes surround the state of Michigan." Natasha knew that it would take too long to write all of that down. She used abbreviations and numbers to save time. She also left out words that weren't important. Her notes looked like this:

NOTES:

4 GL around Mich.

Taking notes as you watch videos is a great way to keep track of important facts.

Your notes only need to make sense to you. However, go back and reread them before you close a video, to make sure you understand what you wrote.

Locate the timeline on your video. This is the bar that tells you how many minutes and seconds have gone by since the video began. This will help you take notes about where in the video you find your information. Now find the pause button. Researchers don't always watch videos straight through. They pause videos when they need to think or write something down. Be patient. It takes a while to make notes about videos.

Now think about how you want to make notes. Some people put information on real or online sticky notes. They rearrange the sticky notes to organize their ideas. Others use real or online index cards. They sort the cards to put ideas in the right order.

Natasha made a chart about her Great Lakes research. She wrote on every other line so she would have room to fill in more information the next time she watched.

Name of Video: On the Shores of the Great Lakes	Creator: Smithsonian	URL: https://www.youtube.com/watch?v=gagnnGKprBE	Length: 2:20

Time	Information Found	My Questions and Ideas
:03	Lighthouse onshore	Is this important?
:09	Michigan surrounded by 4 GL	What is the 5th?
:25	So much water—can't see across	These lakes = big!

Look and listen to your video. As Natasha was researching the Great Lakes of Michigan, she saw waves, trees on the shore, and animals. In the opening seconds of the video, she saw a lighthouse. She wrote that down, even though the person talking in the video didn't mention the lighthouse.

Natasha heard lots of facts as she wrote. This information was just as important as the things she saw. However, don't write down information if you can tell right away that it isn't helpful.

Once you have your notes, you are on your way to creating a great project. You could use the information you found to write a report, give a presentation, or even make a video of your own. Good luck, video detective. Enjoy your search!

To get a copy of this activity, visit www.cherrylakepublishing.com/activities.

Try This

Copy this chart into your notebook and fill it in as you watch one of the videos you picked out in the previous chapter. Remember to skip lines so you have room to add information later!

Name of Video:	Creator:	URL:	Length:

Time	Information Found	My Questions and Ideas

STOP!
Don't write in the book!

Glossary

browser **(BROU-zur)** a computer program that lets you find and look through Web pages or other data

ranking **(RANG-king)** putting items in order from top to bottom, first to last, or most to least important

research **(REE-surch)** a study or investigation in a particular field, usually to learn new facts or to solve a problem

search engine **(SURCH EN-jin)** a Web site that allows you to search other sites for information by entering search terms

strategies **(STRAT-i-jeez)** clever plans for achieving a goal

topics **(TAH-piks)** subjects of discussions, studies, lessons, speeches, or pieces of writing

Find Out More

BOOKS

Range, Ellen. *Take Note! Taking and Organizing Notes*. Ann Arbor, MI: Cherry Lake Publishing, 2014.

Truesdell, Ann. *Find the Right Site*. Ann Arbor, MI: Cherry Lake Publishing, 2012.

WEB SITES

Kentucky Virtual Library

www.kyvl.org/kids/p3_notes/notes.html

Learn more note-taking strategies.

Toronto Public Library—KidsSpace: Research Skills

http://kidsspace.torontopubliclibrary.ca/research.html

Learn more about the research process.

Index

About the Author

Kristin Fontichiaro teaches at the University of Michigan School of Information. She loves to search for new information and has written more than 20 books for kids, teachers, and librarians.